**Live With Purpose: Creating Positive, Lasting Change**
Your Handbook To Creating A Vision in Alignment
With Your Life Purpose

Nathalie Virem

LIVE WITH PURPOSE

Copyright © 2016 by Nathalie Virem

All rights reserved. No part of this book may be reproduced or transmitted in any manner whatsoever without written permission from the author, except in the case of brief quotations embodied in critical articles and reviews.

The information contained in this book is intended to be educational and not for diagnosis, prescription, or treatment of any health disorders, or as a substitute for financial planning. This information should not replace consultation with a competent healthcare or financial professional. The content of this book is intended for use as an adjunct to a rational and responsible program prescribed by a healthcare practitioner or financial professional. The author is in no way liable for any misuse of the material.

## Library of Congress Cataloging-in-Publication Date

Nathalie Virem

Live With Purpose: Creating Positive, Lasting Change

**ISBN:** 978-0-692-57470-6

Author photograph: Carlo Bistolfi

In loving memory of my mother, the ultimate high-value spirit, and beautiful souls yet to be born, my children.

## How can I help?

Hi. My name is Nathalie Virem,
and I'm here to help you find your purpose.

I work with entrepreneurs and world-changers to create what's yet to come, to change the world and to redefine humankind.

Do you want to break the mold?

When others follow "what is," do you look for "what if"?

You don't doubt you will change the world.

Freethinkers are the catalysts for evolution.

There are those who doubt you; prove them wrong.

You hold the key to a better world.

Together, let's make quantum leaps, access new dimensions and raise consciousness.

Live with purpose.

Because purpose is the only thing about us that will never die.

Nathalie Virem

**FREE BONUS VIDEO: "LIVE WITH PURPOSE"** Have you ever felt like there was more you could be doing with your life? Let's start this journey together: www.nathalievirem.com/work-with-nathalie. Video: LIVE WITH PURPOSE

**FOREWORD**

Nathalie Virem is THE catalyst of change. She has studied the greatest recent visionaries leading unusual successful businesses and has collected the best life and business knowledge based on hard evidence. She has an important message for the business world and their leaders, one that will change the way we think, behave and innovate. As an accomplished entrepreneur, I was impressed by Nathalie's research and findings. Her ideas on how purpose helps leaders and organizations find long-term success are very forward thinking. I highly recommend this remarkable book as a guide to fulfill your calling and make a bigger impact in the world.

Dr. Frumi Rachel Barr, entrepreneur and author of *A CEO's Secret Weapon: How to Accelerate Success*.

**Special thanks:**

To Angela Varela for your support and guidance with the launch of this book and for your faith in me.

**Live With Purpose:
Creating Positive, Lasting Change**

# Contents

**INTRODUCTION — WHY PURPOSE SHOULD MATTER** .............. 10

**CHAPTER 1 — TODAY** ................................................................ 13
    I. Reassessing Your Life ................................................ 14
    II. Who Are You .............................................................. 16
    III. Gratitude ................................................................... 19

**CHAPTER 2 — CREATIVITY** ...................................................... 21
    I. What Do You Want. ................................................... 22
    II. Why Do You Want What You Want. ........................ 26

**CHAPTER 3 — WHY ARE YOU HERE** ...................................... 29
    I. Fulfillment ................................................................... 30
    II. Values .......................................................................... 33
    III. Personal Purpose ..................................................... 36

**CHAPTER 4 — WHY YOUR BUSINESS EXISTS** ....................... 41
    I. Business Purpose (Why) ........................................... 42
    II. Business Mission (What) and Strategy (How) ....... 45
    III. How Why You Are Here Aligns with Why Your Business Exists ..................................................... 46

**CHAPTER 5 — SUCCESSFUL VISIONARIES, PURPOSE AND POSITIVE, LASTING CHANGE** ...................... 49
    I. The Theory of "The Golden Circle" .......................... 50
    II. Successful Visionaries. ............................................. 53
    III. Their Business Purpose ........................................... 56
    IV. How They Changed the World with Purpose ....... 58

**CHAPTER 6 — GOALS** ................................................................ 61
    I. Action ........................................................................... 62
    II. Taking the First Step ................................................. 65
    III. Creating Long-Lasting Changes ............................. 67

CHAPTER 7 — MASTER YOUR MIND ........................................ 71
    I.   Self-Esteem ................................................................ 72
    II.  Self-Confidence ......................................................... 75
    III. Fear of Failure & Stress ............................................. 78
    IV. Courage & Vulnerability ............................................ 81
    V.   Mind Mastering ......................................................... 84

CHAPTER 8 — POSITIVE, LASTING CHANGE ........................... 87
    I.   Success ...................................................................... 88
    II.  Quantum Leaps ......................................................... 91
    III. Giving Back ............................................................... 93

CONCLUSION — LIVE WITH PURPOSE ................................... 95
ACKNOWLEDGEMENTS ............................................................ 97

# INTRODUCTION — WHY PURPOSE SHOULD MATTER

**Why Purpose Should Matter to Visionaries**

Live with purpose: How successful visionaries use purpose — as a disruptive and ethical aim — to create positive, lasting change in the world.

In this book, we'll address why purpose is important to visionaries and world-changers.

The relationship between purpose and positive, lasting change has long been a central and contentious debate in literature. In researching this book, I've taken some suppositions from the theory of "The Golden Circle," described in *Start With Why* (Simon Sinek, 2009), in order to review the link between purpose and positive, lasting change in the world.

Based on my research, this book will study the role of some of the greatest visionaries of this 21$_{st}$ century's contributions to society and will provide findings in the significant and positive correlation between purpose and positive, lasting change, proving how purpose helps guarantee success and sustainability.

In 2014, I was going through some heartbreaking times. I was in Spain — where I was born and raised — for several months to be with my mother, who was spending her last days of life in home palliative care. She fought breast cancer for 16 years and was diagnosed with bone metastasis three years prior to passing.

During this trying time, it was as if my mother's suffering and near-ending life was reflecting on my own. I realized that I wasn't living the life I wanted. I didn't even know what I wanted, and I was painfully unfulfilled with my current life choices and situation.

Death being certain for all of us, I hit a breaking point and decided to take action toward achieving my hopes and dreams.

I started watching inspirational videos online and reading self-help books to help me find and better myself. I spent time thinking about who I was, what my values were, what my strengths and weaknesses were, what I wanted in life, and why I wanted it. I hired a career coach who helped me discover my passion for coaching. And I started taking small steps toward my transformation as a whole. Changes in my life appeared in many ways and forms and were aligned with my core values. As I transformed myself for the better, the opportunities appeared and multiplied themselves. Each step of the way offered new opportunities. And each one of these opportunities was bigger and more challenging than the previous one. As I embraced taking action toward them with courage, I was able to multiply my steps while making them bigger and faster. By February of 2015, I completed formal training as a coach through the world-renowned Coaches Training Institute (CTI). I launched my coaching business and website, which is what feeds my heart and spirit today. Purpose found me as I embraced life challenges as opportunities to make choices that honored my values.

This has been an amazing journey, with ups and downs — and downs and ups. I am grateful for everything and astonished by what I've accomplished so far. Sometimes clarity and purpose come from the tests life presents you. In my case, I know my mother opened this door for me, which I am incredibly thankful for. The reason I'm thankful for such a heartbreaking journey is because I am now clear on where I am heading, on my life purpose, and how that purpose reflects in my business like a mirror. I am in control and fulfilled. I know I am headed in the right direction and making meaningful choices every day. I now realize when it is time for me to go, I can look back to see how much I've accomplished, and smile.

Today, I blend my abilities, expertise and experience in my coaching process, which is designed to teach and support my clients all over the world to live with purpose.

If you feel:
- You are living a life without direction, belief, purpose or cause
- Frustrated and incomplete
- Unsure of why you are here or why your business exists
- Unclear on what you aim to achieve in your life, whether it's personal, professional or spiritual
- Life is presenting you with challenges...

... then this book — its knowledge and exercises — will be tremendously valuable.

Because, you know you will spend your days accomplishing what you truly want to ultimately find eternal fulfillment. You know the purpose of life is a life with purpose, and nothing feels as good as living with purpose. You know that once purpose comes to you and you realize your mission, you will find lasting joy.

Now, while every path to achieving a purpose-driven life is unique, some have harder or longer journeys than others. No matter where you are in life, achieving a life with purpose can be done. Whatever your current situation may be, I'd like you to approach every day with simple and easy-to-integrate strategies guaranteed to help you succeed in creating positive, lasting change in the world.

# CHAPTER 1 — TODAY

### I. Reassessing Your Life

To live with purpose, evaluate your current situation. Start by asking yourself these three questions: If a day has 24 hours, what do you spend most of your time on? What do you spend most of your money on? How do you feel about it?

Remember: You have the choice to do what you want to do and to be who you want to be.

Whatever you put into the universe, it is given back to you. Your energy flows in the direction of where you focus your attention. The more you concentrate on or envision the feeling of what you want, the more the universe will return your energy in that same direction.

Start spending your time, money and energy on the things you want rather than the ones you think you need. If there are areas in your life you spend too much time, money or energy on that don't serve you, STOP!

Reassess your priorities by filling in the "Wheel of Life," created by The Coaches Training Institute (www.strategic-solutions-coaching.com/wheel-of-life).

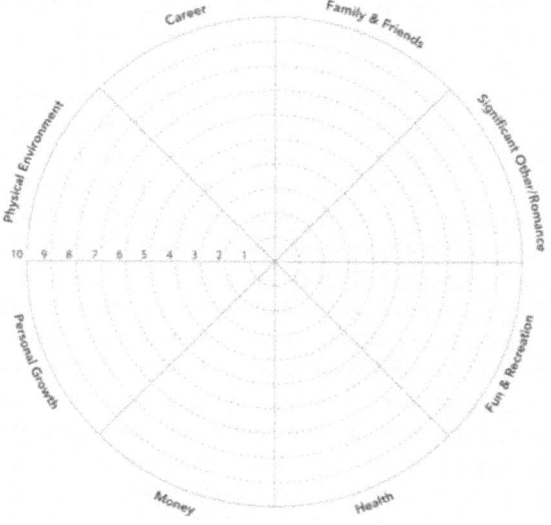

The eight sections in the Wheel of Life represent different aspects of your life. Seeing the center of the wheel as 1 and the outer edges as 10, rank your level of satisfaction with each life area by drawing a straight or curved line to create a new outer edge. The new perimeter represents the wheel of your life. If this were a real wheel, how bumpy would the ride be?

Now that you have assessed your current situation with the "Wheel of Life," it's time to make better choices by focusing on the areas where you want more out of life, while letting go of the ones where you want less.

**FREE BONUS VIDEO: "HOW TO REASSESS YOUR LIFE"**

Life Booster #1 helps you evaluate where you are today. In this video you'll:
- Determine how fulfilled you are with your choices today
- Reassess your priorities
- Focus on the areas you want more from while letting go of the ones you want less of
- Gain clarity and feel happier

Go to www.nathalievirem.com/blog
Life Booster #1: HOW TO REASSESS YOUR LIFE

## II. Who Are You

Most of us spend our days getting to know ourselves. The human being is a special species. Some may even say we never really fully understand who we are.

Getting to know who you are is very important. Since the 1970s, research has supported "self-awareness" as a key trait of successful leaders. A study done by Green Peak Partners and Cornell University of 72 executives with revenues of $50 million to $5 billion revealed "a high self-awareness score was the strongest predictor of overall success."

You may not know everything about yourself, since you are in constant motion and change. It's critical to take the time to get to know yourself and to check in with yourself often to adjust your perception of who you are at the moment.

Your life experiences mold and form who you are today. Your past thoughts, feelings and actions define who you have become. Truly getting to know yourself takes time and requires energy, reflection and self-discovery.

Take the time to assess who you are now. Come back to it in a few months. Re-evaluate that person again. Am I still the same? Where have I changed? What do I want to be more or less of in the next couple months? Once you do that work and understand who you are, your life can take the shape you want it to be.

Take the time to answer these questions:
What are your strengths, talents and gifts?
What areas can you enhance?
What makes you unique and irresistible?
What do you want to bring to others?
Who do you want to be?
What are you passionate about? What inspires and motivates you?

To help you get to know yourself and to define who you want to become, consider completing these exercises:

1. Complete a personality test. The widely used Myers-Briggs Type Indicator® (MBTI®) — based on the work of Carl Jung — can help you get to know yourself. It can help you understand how you deal with your energy, how you learn information, how you make decisions and how you deal with the world. Go to www.mbtionline.com to take the test. There is also the Riso-Hudson Enneagram Type Indicator (RHETI) test, an independent, scientifically validated tool that can help you in the process of self-discovery. To take this test, go to www.enneagraminstitute.com.

2. Ask your friends, family and co-workers how they perceive you. Asking others how they perceive you can be very insightful and can give you information you haven't thought of obtaining.

3. Get your Vedic birth chart done. Vedic astrology can help you understand your strengths, weaknesses and desires, as well as your capacity to accomplish what you desire. It will provide you with valuable insight about your spiritual evolution, happiness and well-being, and answers about your Life Purpose, Prosperity, Pleasure and Spiritual Liberation.

4. Perform regular self-checks. Spend 10 minutes each day this week thinking and writing about who you are and how you'd like to come across to others.

5. Compare the information you have gathered in the previous exercises and see what feels right and comes often.

6. Read the book *The Brand You 50* by Tom Peters. This book will help you build your personal brand by getting to know who you are, what you stand for and what makes you special, resulting in how to better stand out and market yourself.

Once you complete these exercises, send me a note at contact@nathalievirem.com and I can provide you with feedback to help you better know yourself.

**FREE BONUS VIDEO: "HOW TO GET TO KNOW YOURSELF"**

This video underlines the importance of getting to know yourself. You'll discover:
- How and why it helps to get to know yourself on a deeper level
- Your strengths
- What makes you unique (Unique Selling Proposition)
- How to use what inspires you to power your life
- Exactly who and how you want to be seen in the world

You'll get powerful tools and tips to move you forward

Go to www.nathalievirem.com/blog
Life Booster #2: HOW TO GET TO KNOW YOURSELF

### III. Gratitude

Practice gratitude. Gratitude is how we should start and end every day. We should also try to remember what we are grateful for during the day.

Why is that important? Clinical trials by psychologist Robert Emmons — who has done extensive research on gratitude — show that being thankful on a regular basis can significantly increase our well-being (for example: reducing stress, improving one's immune system, lowering blood pressure, facilitating sleep) and life satisfaction (such as happiness).

Therefore, be grateful for what you already have. Feel the feelings of gratitude to attract more good things!

Gratitude doesn't only include the material things you are happy to have; it also includes your challenges, issues or problems. It sometimes even includes wake-up calls. Gratitude is everything that affects you and the ones you love.

When being grateful, you are acknowledging and embracing what surrounds you, your circumstances, situations, opportunities and threats. Your environment consists of things you sometimes can or cannot control, but it is up to you to decide how you want to act on it. When being grateful, you take the next logical step to maintain, improve or change the outcomes in your life. When being grateful, you remind yourself daily how great life is and how lucky you are to be alive one more day.

Practice on a daily basis by following the steps below:

Think of the things that you are grateful for, whether they are material, people, nature, animals, spiritual, personal, professional, etc.

Write down at least 10 things you are grateful for every day. Good or bad, remember gratitude is all of the above. Look at your life and make a list of what you are grateful for today.

For example:

I'm grateful to be alive.
I'm grateful to be healthy.
I'm grateful to be an entrepreneur.
I'm grateful for the people I love.
I'm grateful to have a roof over my head.
I'm grateful for the challenges I am overcoming with my coaching practice.
I'm grateful for the job I have.

And so on...

## CHAPTER 2 — CREATIVITY

### I. What Do You Want

Science has proven that our consciousness is strongly connected to our material world. You can have whatever you want. You attract everything you have in your life because you are the creator and inventor of your own world. To start the creation process, develop in your mind a clear mental image of what you want.

Here is a ritual you can practice on a daily basis. You can do this when you wake up, before you go to bed or during a break. Close your eyes for several minutes. Visualize having what you want and experience the feelings you are sensing as if you already have what you want.

1. ASK for what you want.
Make a list of what you want (write it down and add images). Create what's called a vision board. Get specific: what job you want to have, what team you want to work with and environment you want to work in, which leader you want to work for, what skills you want to use in your job, how much you want to make, and what benefits you want to receive. Google and copy images that you love, that inspire you. Save images of your wants — of the car you desire, the house you dream of, the kind of relationship you aspire to, the places you want to travel to — and look at them regularly. You can change what you ask for at any time. You can redefine wishes as you go.

Ask the universe for it out loud. For example: "I am healthy." Repeat what you want out loud several times until you are very clear about what you want.

As Einstein said, "Imagination is everything. It is the preview of life's coming attractions."

2. VISUALIZE and FEEL.
Dr. Denis Waitley, a noted psychologist who trained NASA astronauts and Olympic athletes, says, "When you visualize, then you materialize." His program was called the Visual Motor Rehearsal. Also, in this same mindset, Deepak Chopra talks

about the power of "attention" and "intention."
The mind can't distinguish whether you're really doing something, or practicing. If there is something you want to manifest into your life, make an effort to get into the mindset of feeling like you already have it.

To help you visualize and feel your want, follow the steps below:

- Find a quiet, dark and private place.
- Listen to soft, meditative music to drop your brain into Alpha wave levels (mental state of relaxed awareness).
- Let go of the past and don't think about the future. Relax into this present moment and visualize the results you want from your vision board each day. Focus your attention on each one of the wishes you listed in the ASK step for a solid 2 to 3 minutes.
- When visualizing, really get into the space of feeling like you already have what you want (Intention). Create a "theater in your mind," and when visualizing the outcome, use as much sound, color and movement as you can. For example: Visualize yourself and your family buying your dream house, and make sure you experience the emotions and physical reaction that come with the feeling of knowing (being certain) that you already have that house. "I have a house with three bedrooms, a beautiful garden with an olive tree, and a beautiful pool where my children play." Repeat, "I have..." several times until you are certain that house belongs to you.

The feeling is what will materialize your desires. If your emotions are positive (hope, love, fulfillment), they are in alignment with what you want. If your emotions consist of frustration, anger or guilt, they will be in alignment with what you don't want. Whatever your feeling is, it will reflect what is in the process of becoming. Therefore, shift your emotions to positive feelings to attract what you want, because what you think and what you feel is always equal to what becomes.

3. TRUST.

Now it's time to surrender, let go and trust. Trust that the universe will manifest what you want. Believe you can have it, believe you deserve it, and believe it is possible for you to obtain it. Detach yourself from the past and from the future. For that, you will need to practice present-moment awareness in all of your actions. One of my favorite books to practice this step is *The Power of Now: A Guide to Spiritual Enlightenment* by Eckhart Tolle.

When completing the TRUST step, you will need to allow the universe to decide the how and the when. The universe will provide what you want in the right form and at the right time, once you are ready for it.

You may also have to acknowledge the blockages that are limiting you from getting what you want before you start the ASK step above. Identifying those blockages and clearing them may be required first. Therefore, before you begin the creation process, take the time to release the disbeliefs in your capability to have and accomplish what you want. For that, ask the universe to guide you in clearing these limiting beliefs. Then embrace the situations the universe will give you. You may have to undergo a difficult time in order to heal from a fear. Trust that whatever the universe brings you, even if it is difficult, will help clean your thoughts and blockages, and create the space for your dreams to exist.

4. PRACTICE GRATITUDE.

Yes, never stop practicing gratitude. Again, be grateful for what you already have, and what you wish to change, improve or overcome. Feel that gratitude to attract more positive things in your life.

**FREE BONUS VIDEO: "HOW TO DREAM BIG"**

In this video, we'll talk about how to define what you want, and put your order in to the Universe, so that, by using this specific process, exactly what you want is magnetically drawn to you. Go ahead, let's help you dream bigger so you can have and experience more in your life!

Go to www.nathalievirem.com/blog
Life Booster #3: HOW TO DREAM BIG

### II. Why Do You Want What You Want

To reach your goals, uncover why you want the things you want and why you do the things you do. It is critical that you understand why.

Why? Why not? What do you have to lose? What's the worst that could happen?

Make sure your why is aligned with your values and purpose (whether it's your personal and/or professional purpose).

We do things because we are passionate about them, because they inspire us. When the excitement is there, it becomes easy to do things. Everything becomes clear and we take the next step naturally, with no effort. It's like we were already preprogrammed to do it when we came to earth.

Simon Sinek applies this theory in the business arena beautifully in his first TEDx Talk on "How Great Leaders Inspire Action."

Great visionaries start with why. "Why" is a way of living and thinking that gives visionaries the ability to inspire change. When a visionary starts with why, he is able to implement his ideas and vision. It's because of the "why," or purpose, that visionaries are able to truly lead.

These visionaries are the ones who stand out, succeed and have a positive, lasting impact on the world. Because they do things differently and think differently, they can inspire the world to change and people to take action.

People follow those visionaries because they believe in what the visionary believes, in their vision, why or purpose. Their motivation to act is personal. They act for the good of something bigger than them not because they have to, but because they want to. They get a sense of purpose that is not attached to an external benefit, like money, for example. It is these followers who are the most loyal followers.

These visionaries tend to be more successful and innovative than others, and they are able to sustain their vision over the long term. They are the ones who change the world positively in the long run.

Finding your why, vision or purpose as a visionary is necessary for success and changing the world. It is a process of self-discovery and self-reflection. It starts with being inspired to do something bigger than you. Finding your why or purpose is actually the easiest part in the process. The hardest part will be staying true to that purpose, cause or belief.

And it is those who build a movement around their purpose — beyond their existence or the existence of their business — who will be able to create positive, lasting change in the world.

**FREE BONUS VIDEO: "HOW TO INSPIRE CHANGE"**

This video talks about the value of 'why' to inspire change:
- Leaders who start with why drive behavior
- People follow them because they believe in what the leader believes, in their vision, why or purpose and want to be part of it
- Leaders and companies who build a movement around their purpose, are able to change the world

Go to www.nathalievirem.com/blog
Life Booster #4: HOW TO INSPIRE CHANGE

## CHAPTER 3 — WHY ARE YOU HERE

### I. Fulfillment

Fulfillment is what feeds your soul, heart and spirit. It is a state of being alive, awake, aware and complete.

People believe they can become more fulfilled when filling the gaps in their lives. If I have this, if I were this, then I would be fulfilled, satisfied. The grass looks greener on the other side! Well, in fact, the grass is greener where you water it.

Look at what you can do today — NOW — to be more fulfilled. What actions can you take right now that will move you toward a fulfilled life?

When you are fulfilled, you are in harmony with the laws of the universe. You are aligned with the source of your energy. This can also exist during difficult times. We can often tap into our inner peace during the biggest struggles of our lives. The path to fulfillment can be rocky, unknown and terrifying at times.

What fulfills you is personal and constantly changing.

I mentioned the Wheel of Life during my first chapter and video. It is a great tool you can use to realign the circumstances of your life toward a more fulfilled state of being.

It is important that you align your life purpose with what you desire and make choices that honor what matters to you the most. To accomplish this, identify your goals and take action and accountability toward your values and life purpose. We will cover this in my next chapter and videos.

If it isn't fun, don't do it. If it doesn't feel right, don't do it.

Here are some tips you can try to start your path to fulfillment:

#1. Give yourself permission to be fulfilled: have fun, laugh, do things that inspire you, meet people you are motivated by, and go to places that make you feel alive.

#2. Change your glasses. Look at things from different perspectives: from the negative angle, from the positive angle, from the superhero point of view, or from the perspective of your heart. You have the power to see things the way you want to see them.

#3. Allow yourself to fail and get back onto your feet. Babies fall over and over but never stop believing or trying until they learn how to walk.

#4. Acknowledge yourself positively. See the strengths you have. Be proud of what you've accomplished. Be proud of who you are.

#5. Be grateful for the things you have, for who you are, for nature, for the good in each person, and for your life. Love your life.

#6. Write down your emotions and feelings. Talk about them with friends and family. Shift your view to release all negativity and blockages or they will reside in your spirit.

#7. Give and share what you can with others. Feed the birds, hand a meal to a homeless person, or give your seat to an older person on the bus.

#8. Look at life as an unlimited field of opportunity. Replace each struggle with a challenge or a lesson learned. Put yourself in situations you've never been in before. Invest in your growth and personal development.

#9. Choose your words carefully and take all negativity, doubt and fear out of your vocabulary.

#10. Like imperfection. Learn how to live with imperfection. The circumstances of your life can always be improved or enhanced.

#11. Celebrate each victory. Celebrate life. Go on a trip once a month. Celebrate with loved ones every week.

#12. Be aware of how you present yourself physically. Stand up straight, with your chest open. Smile. Look into people's eyes when you address or acknowledge them.

#13. Allow yourself to have bad days and feel down. It's OK! Life will challenge you to deserve fulfillment. The tough times life tests you with here and there will only enhance your need to be fulfilled.

As I mentioned in the introduction of this book, you know you will spend your days accomplishing what you truly want to ultimately find eternal fulfillment. You know the purpose of life is a life with purpose, and nothing feels as good as living with purpose. You know that once purpose comes to you and you realize your mission, you will find lasting joy.

**FREE BONUS VIDEO: "HOW TO FEEL MORE FULFILLED"**

When you are fulfilled, your life has deeper meaning, greater impact and can even more strongly impact the world around you.
Discover the secrets of feeling more:
- Alive
- Awake
- Aware
- Complete
- Fulfilled

Go to www.nathalievirem.com/blog
Life Booster #5: HOW TO FEEL MORE FULFILLED

## II. Values

To live with purpose, unveil your values. As a leader, aligning your values will help you feel more fulfilled.

Because your values determine what's most important in your life today, what you value the most -your values will give you purpose.

Values are personal and constantly evolving. They represent who you are today, now in the present moment.

They represent the characteristics of your life lived from the heart. Your values are why you are who you are today and why it matters to you. What you value is in harmony with your heart, soul and spirit.

Values are intangible. They are how you feel, not what you have or do. They come from the heart and reflect on you like a mirror.

Values will present themselves in your life experiences. On some occasions, you may dishonor your values and on other occasions, you may fight for them. That's OK; don't be too hard on yourself. Just be aware of it and try to rectify it. Ideally, you will not compromise your values, because they will help you determine the best decisions to make in life.

It may take time to find your values. Since they show up over time, it is unlikely that you will obtain a complete and accurate list in one shot.

Finally, because your value system is a powerful tool in helping you see your purpose, cause or belief, it is important that you identify them prior to concretizing your life purpose. Values will point you toward choices aligned with your life purpose and will bring you fulfillment. They will also guide you whenever you come across a major crossroads or decision, or if you get off track.

Discover 3 simple steps to clearly understanding your own values

1. The things you can't live without. The things that make you the happiest.
2. The things you can't live with, that you regret the most.
3. A breakthrough moment in your life, when life was particularly fulfilling or challenging.

Examples of values can look like this:

- Vision / Purpose / Change
- Trust / Integrity / Inspiration
- Empowerment / Transformation / Achievement
- Spirituality / Inner Harmony / Personal Development

Here is a fun exercise about values:

1. List your values.
2. Rank the top six. You can change the order at any time. By doing that, you will raise your awareness about the values that matter most in your life.
3. Determine how you are currently honoring these values by ranking them on a scale from 1 to 10.
4. Remind yourself of your top values daily and make sure they are aligned with your vision for yourself. Keep in mind those that fulfill you and that you are proud of.

If you are struggling with getting clear on your values or any of the other concepts we've talked about so far, I'd love to support you in achieving that.

You can apply for a free Purpose Discovery Session where we will work together to:
- Uncover what is blocking you from achieving clarity of purpose
- Get clear on what you would like to be experiencing instead
- Create a step-by-step plan to get you there

You'll come away from this session with great tools and techniques to continue to get even more clear on your purpose and vision, so you can achieve a life that's a great legacy for others.

Apply right now - go here to complete a short questionnaire: www.nathalievirem.com/application

**FREE BONUS VIDEO: "HOW TO FIND YOUR VALUES"**

This video will help you get clear on your values. Your values will point you to your life purpose. You will identify, prioritize your values and assess how well you are currently honoring your values today.
I will also share with you three simple ways to help you identify your values.

Go to www.nathalievirem.com/blog
Life Booster #6: HOW TO FIND YOUR VALUES

### III. Personal Purpose

Philosophers have been writing about purpose for several centuries. Once the importance of purpose was realized in more recent years, scientists and the world of business started researching the topic. Today, numerous scientific studies have shown that having a purpose in life improves our health and brain function, increases our life expectancy, reduces our stress and can even lead to a greater happiness over time.

Identifying your life purpose is a process. It is a path, not a destination. It is a work in progress. While walking this path, you will come across situations and people who will detour you, or on the contrary, will get you closer to your life purpose.

It takes time and comes when it comes. Learn to enjoy the journey until you have the big breakthrough that reveals your life purpose.

Finding your life purpose can seem intimidating at first, but it can easily take one or two simple steps to help get you started. There are several ways to begin: reading books that inspire you, learning from people you admire, spending time on self-reflection and self-discovery, keeping a journal, interviewing those who exemplify a fulfilled life, or simply, truly caring for others. There is a reason why they are part of your life today. Your life purpose is your calling. It's the hunger that fills your heart and spirit, and the pain you are capable of easing in yourself and others.

You live with purpose when you use your gifts. If you are using the unique talents life gave you, the experiences you are confronted with and the teachings they offer will help you form your life purpose.

Living with purpose is intentional. Your purpose is not accidental. There is a reason why it is your purpose. And you are the only one who can discern your purpose. Nobody else can do it for you. Remember: You have the right and responsibility to live with purpose. The purpose of life is a life with purpose.

Discovering and then realizing your life purpose is the key to fulfillment. When you clearly know what you want in life (whether it is spiritual, material, personal, professional, physical or emotional), you will spend your days accomplishing your purpose to ultimately find eternal joy. Set clear goals and have the courage to act on them.

So, follow your purpose, not what society tells you is necessary to achieve happiness. Let go of what doesn't resonate with your heart.

Study others, especially those who inspire you to be wiser. Study yourself to be enlightened, to raise your awareness and consciousness. What gifts do you have? What talents? Apply them in the direction of your life purpose.

The key to success is a life with purpose — where you put yourself in a state of joy and immense inner happiness.

Your mission's purpose is whatever you decide it is. Ask yourself: What is your purpose in this life?

What is the best way to uncover your life purpose? You can enhance the probability of being united with your life purpose by:

- Performing guided inner journeys (envisioning), especially those related to your inner child. To help you achieve this, write down what brought you immense joy as a kid.
- Practicing self-exploration: Decide how you want to interact with others by answering how you would like other people to view you in relation to themselves. For example, ask yourself: What would you do to be a better person for them?

- Learning from others: Identify three people who inspire you and read their biographies or watch online videos of them.
- Practicing shamanic work, such as breath work like rebirthing or Kundalini yoga, can help you clear blockages and get answers about your life purpose.
- Taking the time to write down your vision statement.
- Taking action. This is so important! To cultivate your life mission, you will need to plant and harvest your goals. Set clear personal, professional and spiritual goals and then have the courage to act on them. It is hard to think your way into finding your life purpose. It is easier to "do" your way into it. The more you act, the more you will become clear on the experiences in your life that form your thinking. Start taking steps toward your goals and trying new things. Stop overthinking whether it will work out or if you should even attempt it. Just do it!
- Saying no to life experiences that don't bring you joy. These activities distract you from your purpose.
- Doing what makes you truly happy. What brings a tremendous amount of joy in your life? By doing what you love, you will be inspired and gain insights into your life purpose.

Clarity in your life purpose will ultimately come through the process of exploring and taking action.

When you complete this chapter, send me an email at contact@nathalievirem.com to let me know what your life purpose is, and I will provide you with feedback that can help you get clear on where you want to go in order to accomplish your life vision and find eternal joy.

**FREE BONUS VIDEO: "HOW TO FIND YOUR LIFE PURPOSE"**

Success is simple when you understand and are in alignment with your life purpose. Once you are clear about why you're here, decisions become simple, your path becomes more obvious, and you can make choices that move you further along that path easily.

On this video you'll discover new ways to integrate your goals with your purpose and be able to reach those goals faster than you ever dreamed possible.

Don't wait - go watch this one right now!

Go to www.nathalievirem.com/blog
Life Booster #7: HOW TO FIND YOUR LIFE PURPOSE

## CHAPTER 4 — WHY YOUR BUSINESS EXISTS

### I. Business Purpose (Why)

The Purpose of a business can be described as its "why." That is, why does the business exist? What is its aim, goal or function? It represents what we see as possible. A business' Purpose is in the origin of its Vision. The Vision also answers why a business exists and what the business aspires to solve for others. It is the desired future state of the business. Therefore, a business' Purpose is also its Vision, or "why."

A business should be motivated in more than just being profitable to explain or validate its existence. In other words, making a profit is a result and not a means to an end. A business purpose should be aligned with a larger and bigger picture, beyond the visionary's vision for himself. It should impact society and the world to some extent. It should heal a pain or solve a problem to improve the quality of life for the general public.

The relationship between purpose and positive, lasting change has long been a central and contentious debate in literature. In researching this book, I have taken some suppositions from the theory of *The Golden Circle* (Simon Sinek, 2009) in order to review the link between purpose and positive, lasting change in the world.

We will see how successful visionaries who start with purpose are able to inspire. And that people follow them not because they have to, but because they want to. Starting with purpose is what separates a successful visionary from the rest.

A business purpose or vision that doesn't take into consideration the larger role that the company plays in the world will not be able to sustain success over time.

Today, research proves that to create positive, lasting change, a business needs to have a clear, defined purpose that is fully understood by its stakeholders. Businesses will only gain followers when it becomes apparent to consumers why that business exists and how it can improve their lives.

Vision gives direction. In fact, the Deloitte Core Beliefs & Culture Survey, conducted in 2013 and 2014, respectively, (http://www2.deloitte.com/us/en/pages/about-deloitte/articles/culture-of-purpose.html) shares some key findings about the impact of purpose on the business world:

1. Organizations that focus beyond profits and instill a culture of purpose are more likely to find long-term success.

2. Ninety-one percent of respondents (both executives and employees) who said their company had a strong sense of purpose also said their company had a history of strong financial performance.

3. Despite the company's findings, employees (68%) and executives (66%) believed that businesses were not doing enough to instill in their culture a sense of purpose aimed at making a positive impact on all stakeholders.

Furthermore, an EY Beacon Institute research report (http://www.ey.com/Publication/vwLUAssets/ey-the-state-of-the-debate-on-purpose-in-business/$FILE/ey-the-state-of-the-debate-on-purpose-in-business.pdf) lists their insights on the "five aspects of how purpose can bring greater strategic impetus and be a guiding force for corporate transformation and long-term value creation." These are:

1. Purpose instills strategic clarity.
2. Purpose channels innovation.
3. Purpose is a force for and a response to transformation.
4. Purpose taps a universal need.
5. Purpose builds bridges.

A visionary should consider how important purpose is for his business and should be fully committed to communicate his business purpose to the world. It is also the visionary's responsibility to ensure that stakeholders completely comprehend the business purpose. This enables stakeholders to evaluate whether the company is a good fit for them before they commit to participating in its purpose.

Therefore, while a business has to be profitable to exist, making a profit is a result. A business should convey a clear purpose or vision in order to thrive and sustain success over time.

For me, my business exists to help leaders, visionaries and entrepreneurs find and align their personal and business purposes, so that they can create positive, lasting change in the world.

What about you? If you need some support on helping you define your business vision, contact me at contact@nathalievirem.com to schedule a complimentary discovery free session, where we would work together to create a clear vision and a step by step plan to reach it.

**FREE BONUS VIDEO: INTERVIEW WITH DR. FRUMI RACHEL BARR "HOW TO START WITH WHY"**

A true entrepreneur, Dr. Frumi Rachel Barr will help you perceive your own 'why' and will share her insights on how 'starting with why' guarantees success and sustainability.

She is the author of A CEO's Secret Weapon: How to Accelerate Success, ranked the top business book of 2012 by ExecRank and with a foreword by her colleague, Simon Sinek, international best-selling author of Start With Why.

Go to www.nathalievirem.com/blog
Interview 11: HOW TO START WITH WHY

## II. Business Mission (What) and Strategy (How)

The business' Mission describes "what" the business is going to do to accomplish that Purpose. It represents the activities the business will perform for society and the world to accomplish its purpose.

To inspire change and succeed over time, it is important for internal and external stakeholders (customers, employees, investors, vendors, the environment, owners and the community in which the business operates) to understand the business' purpose as well as its mission. And it is essential that all parties understand how the business' vision and mission will affect them, and how they can affect that particular vision and mission in return.

The business strategy defines how the business will accomplish its Mission. It includes the methods the business will use to achieve its Mission.

The strategy is defined in the process or value proposition.

The business' Mission also needs to be ethical and responsible to ensure profitability over time. The price to be paid for not behaving in a socially responsible way can be the key to a company's existence. Today, consumers are well informed, making it extremely difficult for a business to hide its actions. A values-based business understands that being profitable is insufficient to ensure its success and motivate people.

### III. How Why You Are Here Aligns with Why Your Business Exists

As a visionary, it is important to realize that your life has a personal and professional purpose. Your personal purpose relates to why you are here, and your professional purpose relates to why your business exists.

As a visionary, you also need to address the question of how your personal and professional purposes align. At the end of the day, both are heavily interconnected, and it will be impossible to see one without seeing the other.

Personal and professional purposes can evolve over time, and both are personal to you. Each of these purposes differs from one person to another. Once you are able to align both, you will enjoy lasting fulfillment. If there is a gap between the two, you may be able to accomplish great things, but you will not be able to create positive, lasting change in the world, nor will you be fully fulfilled. Sooner or later, you will suffer from this realization.

You will know you are in alignment with your personal and professional purposes once you become conscious and integrate everything you do, whether personal or professional, fully into your life. Your personal and professional purposes will eventually merge into one.

Then, your purposes become one. They will be in alignment with your spirit, and your goals and aspirations will be one as well. At that point, whatever your purpose is — personal and/or professional — it will create positive, lasting change in the world. There will be quality in what you do, and you will be able to make a significant impact on the world.

Live a life with purpose and be true to yourself. Success comes from within. When you speak your true inner voice, and when that inner voice is real, you can only succeed. When you are able to align your personal and professional purposes with your values and heart, the world will eventually change.

Instead of putting your attention into the things that seem promising — from a personal and professional perspective — put your undivided attention into the things that resonate within your heart. Trust your intuition (or in simpler terms, trust your gut), and everything will fall into place.

**FREE BONUS VIDEO: INTERVIEW WITH DR. JAMES MELLON "HOW TO MASTER LIFE"**

Dr. James Mellon is the Spiritual Leader of the Global Truth Center, a Center for Spiritual Living in North Hollywood, California.

In this video, you will learn to:
- Know you are creative
- Remember you are the creator of your life
- Listen to your true inner voice and intuition
- Accomplish your purpose in life

Go to www.nathalievirem.com/blog
Interview 14: HOW TO MASTER LIFE

**CHAPTER 5 — SUCCESSFUL VISIONARIES, PURPOSE AND POSITIVE, LASTING CHANGE**

### I. The Theory of "The Golden Circle"

The relationship between purpose and positive, lasting change has long been a central and contentious debate in literature. This book takes some suppositions from the theory of "The Golden Circle" described in *Start With Why* (Simon Sinek, 2009), in order to review the link between purpose and positive, lasting change in the world.

Simon Sinek's Golden Circle theory is based on the Golden Ratio concept. The Golden Ratio idea is a mathematical relationship that has been used in the past by many mathematicians, architects, biologists and so on.

Simon's Golden Circle provides evidence on the positive results visionaries can obtain if they start their ventures by asking why.

This theory explains why some visionaries and businesses are able to influence consumers more than those who don't start with why. When using why, visionaries are able to inspire and to do so in the long term.

Therefore, Simon's perspective is useful in understanding how a visionary can inspire and create loyal followers by turning an idea into a social movement that can change the world.

When picturing The Golden Circle, visualize a circle made up of three parts, much like a bull's-eye: The "why" is at the center, the "how" is in the middle, and the "what" is found in the outer ring of the circle. The Golden Circle theory starts from the inside and moves out of that sphere: from **"why," to "how" to "what."** Simon believes that every company knows "what" they do (their products, services, job functions...), some know "how" they do "what" they do (how their processes or propositions are different or better), and very few visionaries know "why" they do "what" they do. By "why," Simon refers to their purpose, cause or belief. That is "why" their business exists.

Those distinct visionaries and their businesses are able to change the world, regardless of the size or industry of the company. Because in his opinion, they all think, act and communicate from the inside out: from "why," to "how" to "what."

Simon uses Apple as an example to describe one's success over time. Having forever changed the way human beings use technology, Apple has attracted loyal followers and proven to remain one of the most innovative companies, year after year.

For example, if Apple started their marketing communications with "what" and "how," the consumer would receive this message: "We make great computers. They're beautifully designed, simple to operate and user-friendly. Want to buy one?"

However, here is how Apple actually communicates: They start with "why." "Everything we do, we believe in challenging the status quo. We believe in thinking differently. The way we challenge the status quo is by making our products beautifully designed, simple to operate and user-friendly. And we happen to make great computers. Want to buy one?" Indeed, most Apple TV ads in the late 90s included a slogan at the end that stated, "Think different."

Because Apple communicates from the inside out by starting with "why," the company is able to inspire. This is a perfect example of The Golden Circle theory: "People don't buy 'what' you do; they buy 'why' you do it."

Sinek sustains that it's not "what" Apple does that distinguishes them. It's "why" they do it, and everything Apple does serves to demonstrate their "why." That is, to challenge the status quo, to think differently.

Their application of the Golden Circle theory is proof Apple was able to change the music industry with their products, despite not having invented most of the technologies behind such devices and stiff competition from others. Their products, while aesthetically pleasing and easy to use, don't always offer the newest and strongest features, yet they still continue to dominate the market.

Starting with "why" allowed Apple to innovate in ways no other competitor could, sometimes even against more qualified competitors or in industries outside their core functions.

The reason why Apple continues to lead in innovation and create lasting change in the world is because since Apple's creation in the late 1970s, its "why" hasn't changed. No matter what products they make or what industry they venture into, no matter "what" they do or "how" they do it, their "why" remains the same. Therefore, if you want to inspire sustainable change over time, start with "why."

Based on the Golden Circle theory, the "what" relates to the human's "rational and analytical thought and language," which is "our newest brain, our homo sapiens brain, our neocortex." On the other hand, the "why" corresponds to our feelings, like trust and loyalty. It is our limbic brain. And the limbic brain is "responsible for all human behavior, all decision-making, and it has no capacity for language," according to Sinek. Therefore, to inspire change or motivate a decision to buy, we need to relate to the human being's limbic brain, and that is the "why." "Why" creates action to buy, followers and loyalty. Starting with "why" is the way to be successful — as a visionary and as a business — and the way to sustain success.

## II. Successful Visionaries

This section of the book will study the role of some of the greatest visionaries of this 21st century's contribution to society.

The criterion used for this study was the research of a few visionaries who are real game changers — who have had a significant and sustainable impact on the world. We will demonstrate how these visionaries are able, when using purpose — as a disruptive and ethical aim — to create positive, lasting change.

One clear example of a successful visionary is Steve Jobs. He was best known as the chairman, co-founder and CEO of Apple, Inc. But he was also one of the major shareholders of Pixar Animation Studios, as well as the founder and CEO of NeXT, Inc. He is one of the greatest visionaries of this century. He revolutionized the world of technology, music and film. He created new industries and new products that were unimaginable at the time, such as downloading songs for just 99 cents each, watching computer-animated films, and being able to put your phonebook, email, music collection, photos and more right in your pocket! He made possible what was yet to come. And he was able to do so because he used purpose.

Steve Jobs was adopted in San Francisco. He briefly attended college, then dropped out of school, travelled to India and studied Buddhism.

Once he returned, he co-founded Apple in 1976. In 1985, Steve Jobs was forced out of Apple due to a conflict of interest with another highly influential executive. When leaving, Steve took a few members with him and founded NeXT. NeXT created WebObjects, an application that was used to build and run its Apple and iTunes Stores. Apple, Inc. acquired the company in 1997, when Jobs became the CEO once again. He then funded Pixar, an innovative company that would produce the first fully computer-animated films in the world, such as *Toy Story*.

When Jobs returned to Apple in 1997, the company was on the verge of bankruptcy. But with Jobs back on board, the company was able to return to profitability. This was made possible because Jobs returned with a purpose, and he embedded the subsequent marketing campaign of Apple with that purpose: "Think different." Every product and innovation Jobs has ever been involved in, whether it was with Apple, NeXT or Pixar, has always been closely linked to Jobs' purpose of thinking differently and defeating the status quo. In 2003, Jobs was diagnosed with a pancreatic tumor, and he died of respiratory arrest due to his cancer in 2011.

Another example is Sergey Brin and Larry Page, known as the Google Duo. The Google founders met at Stanford in 1995, and in 1996 they built a search engine they initially named BackRub. In 1997, they decided to change the name to Google. The company has since created thousands of jobs all around the world and generated billions of dollars in revenue. Today, the founders of Google are said to be America's newest billionaires.

In 2004, the company had an initial public offering (IPO), allowing them to sell stocks as a public company. Along with going public, Google manifested its motto "Don't be evil" under the owners 'belief that "in the long term, we will be better served — as shareholders and in all other ways — by a company that does good things for the world even if we forgo some short-term gains. This is an important aspect of our culture and is broadly shared within the company." The IPO made many employees millionaires. Since then, Google continues to innovate, provide free products to the world (Gmail, Google Apps, Google Earth and Google Maps, and so on), and change the world. Furthermore, its owners Page and Brin top the richest people in the world list, still hold a substantial portion of Google, and maintain voting power in one of the most disruptive and innovative companies of the world.

And finally, Elon Musk is a very successful visionary today. Musk was born in South Africa in 1971. By the time Musk had turned 24, he had started his first company, Zip2, an online city guide for newspapers. In 1999, at just 28, he sold Zip2 for $307 million. That same year, Musk formed X.com (which is known today as PayPal). In 2002, eBay acquired PayPal for $1.5 billion in stock and Musk founded SpaceX9. Two years later, he invested in Tesla Motors. In 2007, SpaceX won a $1.6 billion contract with NASA. In 2008, the same year he became the CEO of Tesla, the company went public. While still under Musk's guidance, Tesla started selling the all-electric Model S in 2012. That same year, SpaceX began its first commercial resupply services mission to the International Space Station for NASA. Elon Musk also founded SolarCity with his cousins in 2006, which is one of the largest solar installation companies in the U.S. today.

### III. Their Business Purpose

As previously said, the Purpose of a business can be described as its "why." That is, why does the business exist? What is its aim, goal or function?

A business' Purpose is in the origin of its Vision. The Vision also answers why a business exists and what problems the business aspires to solve for others. It is the desired future state of the business.

Therefore, a business' Purpose is also its Vision, or "why."

Let's take the example of Steve Jobs. Steve Jobs' personal purpose was "to remove the barrier of having to learn" through technology and "to challenge the status quo." His purpose, or calling, was so clear to him, that even during the hardest times of his life, (including when he was fired from Apple, his own company), he was able to create positive, lasting change in the world. Because as he mentioned during his Commencement Speech to Stanford's 2005 graduating class, he was still in love, he was still on track with his purpose in life. And nothing can stop you from succeeding and creating positive, lasting change when you are aligned with your purpose. Your personal purpose is intimately connected to why your business exists. And Steve Jobs' personal purpose — "to remove the barrier of having to learn" — was mirroring why his businesses existed.

Apple exists "to make tools for the mind that advance humankind." Everything Apple does is supported by the belief in "challenging the status quo." They believe in thinking differently. And Pixar exists "to develop computer-animated feature films with memorable characters and heartwarming stories that appeal to audiences of all ages," according to their mission statement. Everything that Apple or Pixar does reflects Steve Jobs' purpose.

Another example is Google. Google's purpose is to "do good things for the world." It is also known that Google's unofficial mission statement is "Don't be evil." As founder Larry Page said, "We have a mantra: don't be evil, which is to do the best things we know how for our users, for our customers, for everyone. So, I think if we were known for that, it would be a wonderful thing."

The founders' personal purpose is incorporated within their company's vision statement: "To organize the world's information and make it universally accessible and useful. "Here again, we can see how the founders' purpose is perfectly aligned with their company's purpose. Ever since Larry Page was a child, he wanted to "do good" for the world; he wanted to change the world.

Google mirrors Larry Page's calling since he was a kid. Founding Google is an image of his aspirations as a human being, just like Apple was for Jobs.

As for Elon Musk, his personal purpose is focused on human beings and their existence. Musk's cause is "to provide humanity with the best future." And here again we see the link between Musk's purpose and his companies' purposes. Tesla's vision statement is to "create the most compelling car company of the 21st century by driving the world's transition to electric vehicles." SpaceX's vision is to "enable multi-planetary human life." And SolarCity's vision is to enable "a cleaner and more affordable alternative to your utility bill."

### IV. How They Changed the World with Purpose

Let's now analyze the positive correlation between purpose and positive, lasting change. That is how purpose helps guarantee positive, lasting change in the world.

It is clear that thanks to Steve Jobs, Apple changed the world. Apple has changed the way we use technology during the past few decades. It has created and invented products that allow us to do things that were inconceivable back then, such as literally being able to put music in your pocket via their mp3 player, the iPod. Now while Apple did not invent the mp3 technology, consumers perceive that they were the ones who changed the music industry. It's not "what" Apple does that distinguishes them, it's "why" they do it. Here is an example of when a company starts with "why": They are able to innovate in ways other companies can't. They are able to access new industries, inspire action to buy, and gain loyal followers, time after time. Since its creation, Apple has formed new industries, created millions of jobs and generated billions of dollars.

The same goes for Pixar. Pixar's innovative creation of computer-animated films forever changed the movie industry. With over 10 feature films, Pixar has generated billions of dollars worldwide.

Steve Jobs is a clear example of how a visionary, when using purpose as a disruptive and ethical aim (by removing the barrier of having to learn through technology and challenging the status quo), can create positive, lasting change in the world.

It is also clear that Google has changed the world positively over time. It changed several industries, such as the search, printing, information, advertising and video industries, among many others.

Today, Google is the most powerful search engine in the world. We no longer rely on going to the library to do extensive research. We no longer need to buy printed books, newspapers or magazines. Google allows us to search online for audio books, eBooks, newspapers, articles, magazines and much more.

Consequently, it has changed the way we educate and inform ourselves.

Another example of how Google has positively changed our lives is through its purchase and further development of YouTube, which allows us to post and share videos from just about any location and recording device for free.

The same goes for mapping. With Google Maps, you can scale maps to fit and find driving directions, and you can also tag or locate services in a certain location. The GPS industry wouldn't be where it is today if it weren't for Google Maps.

The advertising industry was also greatly affected by Google. In 2000, Google started selling ads based on users' searches, changing the way advertising firms reached out to different demographics.

Finally, another great invention of Google is Android, their mobile phone operating system that launched in 2008. Since then, Android has been a huge success, with great features and millions of followers around the world.

These are just some of the ways Google, again with purpose — don't be evil and do good things for the world — has been able to create positive, lasting change in the world. And this is perhaps just the beginning; Google has many new innovations in the works that may continue to shape the future of our lives.

Finally, Elon Musk's companies Tesla and SolarCity have changed the energy industries with more sustainable and cleaner energy. And his rocket company SpaceX is changing the world of space exploration with the possibility of extending life beyond Earth. His goal is to colonize Mars with humans within the next century.

Today, SpaceX is working on a new spacecraft that will bring humans to Mars. The Tesla Model S has changed the automotive industry with the highest ever Consumer Reports rating and the highest safety features. Today, Tesla is preparing for the launch of their Model 3, which makes clean transportation affordable for more consumers. As of April 2016, there were already 400,000 pre-orders. And SolarCity is a major installer of solar panels in the U.S. and is currently partnering with Tesla to create the Powerwall, a home battery product powered by solar panels that will generate energy for homes after the sun goes down.

There are so many visionaries throughout history who have changed the world through purpose. Mother Teresa -who was awarded the Nobel Peace Prize in 1979 and died in 1997- believed in helping the dying and sick. Her Missionaries of Charity expanded to hundreds of countries and consisted of thousands of sisters. Scientist Albert Einstein changed the way we see the world and the universe to date with his theories of matter, energy, light and gravity. We can easily extend this list to many other visionaries, who -through the use of purpose-were able to perceive a different world, a world not quite perceivable for most of us.

In conclusion, we can see how great visionaries are able to have a significant and long-term impact on the world when they use purpose as a disruptive and ethical aim. The suppositions used from Sinek's "The Golden Circle" have helped review the link between purpose and positive, lasting change in the world.

**CHAPTER 6 — GOALS**

I. **Action**

Once you have a clear understanding of who you are, and of what your values and life purpose are, it's time to create an action plan. A vision and goals.

Your vision is what you want your life to look like in one year, five years, or even 10 years from now. Who do you want to become? What do you want to do? Who are your friends? Where do you want to live? What does your love life look like? Get specific. Utilize the vision board you created in Chapter Two
— Creativity: "How to Dream Big (or WHAT Do You Want)," Step 1: "Ask."

Your goals will be the small steps that will move you forward toward your vision. It represents what you see as possible for you, others and the world. Create 3 to 5 goals every three months. Then take three actions daily toward these goals. Make your goals specific and detailed, and then track them. Don't get discouraged if you can't achieve what you planned to on time. Everything is in divine order. You will get to it when you are ready for it and when it's time.

Here is a good way to start:

#1. Pick a subject you'd like to work on. Choose a topic aligned with your values and life purpose or why you are here.

#2. Try to understand how you are seeing it now. The way you feel about it or the viewpoint you have on this matter today.

#3. Redefine what you see as possible about this subject from different angles. This is the time you identify all the imaginable perspectives, angles or possibilities you can see the matter from: the heart, the hero, the positive, the not-so-good, the creative perspective, etc. Zoom in and out of each one of those perspectives. See how you feel about each perspective and what it tells you: perhaps that you should be patient, that you should take action or that it's the first time to plant the seeds before collecting a reward. The goal is to look at it through different glasses and push the edge of these possibilities. Move from one perspective to another. Try to embody, envision and feel each one of those perspectives. Allow your body to represent that perspective and your posture will naturally incorporate its inherent attitude and beliefs. Each perspective will have its own attitude and belief.

#4. Narrow the list. Once you have gone through several scenarios, choose a perspective or a combination of several of them. Which lenses do you want to wear? What perspective is more resourceful, creative and will provide more action? Which one — or ones — will you choose and why? Make sure it is positive and aligned with your life purpose and values. Stay true to yourself and who you are. Close your eyes and see how it feels. If you feel expanded or elevated, it's a good perspective. If you feel closed up and your body is retracting, you probably shouldn't go for this perspective. See if the energy flows in your body.

#5. Check in and choose. Finally, if this perspective feels good, identify how you can change and what alternative course of actions you can take. Don't take actions based on fear, temporary circumstances or obligation. Make sure you are celebrating your values and life purpose in your choices. You are free, creative and in control of your life.

Once that's done, commit to ways to be and actions to take and be held accountable for. What will you be saying yes to? And what will you be saying no to? How committed are you to doing this? What do you want to be accountable for today, this week, and this month?

Once you decide on a course of action, check on your progress periodically. What worked and what didn't? What did you learn? Where do you want to go next?

It is important to take action. Taking action teaches you how to dance in the rain and navigate through life, which enables you to make choices that are in alignment with your energy. It also allows you to move forward toward your life purpose.

Every moment is an opportunity to make the right choice for you. It is an opportunity to say yes to something that resonates with you. It is an opportunity to say no to something that deviates you from why you are here and your life purpose.

Learn to make decisions fast to avoid pain. Decision-making is like a muscle needed to exercise. It requires that you look inside and meditate to make choices and take action. You can't control your circumstances, but you can choose how you act on them!

**FREE BONUS VIDEO: "HOW TO TAKE ACTION"**

This video will help you create an action to accomplish your vision. Learn how to:
- Create goals and an action plan
- Prioritize your objectives
- Experience accountability to accomplish vision
- Make choices aligned with your values and life purpose.

Go to www.nathalievirem.com/blog
Life Booster #8: HOW TO TAKE ACTION

## II. Taking the First Step

Don't leave for tomorrow what you can do today. Don't second-guess your gut feeling. When the opportunity comes, take it!

Creating what's yet to come starts with nothing. From nothing starts something. That is the first step, and then the second one, and so forth. As you keep on taking incremental action to change, the opportunities come and multiply themselves until you start making what I call quantum leaps.

Therefore, it's important that you do take the first step, even if you can't yet see the whole. Even if the future is unknown and unclear at the time.

Start somewhere; take the first step that you can take today. In order to avoid becoming overwhelmed, divide your bigger goals into small action bites. Then take a small action right now, followed immediately by the next action, and the next one. Taking smaller actions will make them easier to tackle, and you'll be more likely to follow through. Once your actions are completed, an opportunity will come, and another one. And where you once thought there were no possibilities, they will appear.

Splitting your bigger goals into smaller actions is the first step, as we saw earlier. If you don't have small actions in place, you cannot take the first step.

Taking the first step every day is vital. Put your thoughts, time, energy and money into the things that are important to you now — today — and that are in tune with your deepest desires.

If you don't know why these goals matter to you, it will be hard to take the first step. Sometimes life circumstances will force you to take the first step (the death of a loved one, etc.).

Decide to take action.
What is the price to pay if you don't take action now, or today? What's the worst that could happen?

Check your body language: Are you sitting up straight, with your heart open, smiling? Don't delay and don't second-guess. When the opportunity comes, and your gut feeling says yes, act.

Don't be scared. If you don't try, you will never attain what you dare to have in life. Be courageous and take the first step today. You can start with nothing and once you take that first step, the impossible becomes possible and the doors open, step by step.

"Take the first step in faith. You don't have to see the whole staircase, just take the first step."

— Martin Luther King, Jr.

**FREE BONUS VIDEO: "HOW TO TAKE THE FIRST STEP"**

This video will help you:

- Take action before the whole path lights up
- Divide your bigger goals into smaller steps
- Accomplish what you can today
- Create new opportunities to help you reach your dreams

Go to www.nathalievirem.com/blog
Life Booster #9: HOW TO TAKE THE FIRST STEP

**III. Creating Long-Lasting Changes**

To transform and make long-lasting changes, become a new person, create new beliefs and habits. Change your body language, your communication, your diet, your thoughts, your spirit, your determination and your questioning. You will need to achieve self-mastery or continuous improvement, growth and evolution. To be successful in the outside world, change your inner self. Remember: "Your thoughts become your actions, become your habits, become your character, and become your destiny."

To transform, create a new environment. Carefully select your environment, the people around you, your house, your car, your work environment, and your social environment. Develop new areas in your life like meditation, finances, communication, self-esteem, self-confidence and neuroscience. Change your environment and you will change yourself.

To transform, you will need to give yourself permission to change. Give yourself permission to live your deepest desires. How much time are you going to wait before you give yourself permission to live the way you want, the way you dreamed of? Give yourself permission to live the life you want and deserve today.

Get clear on what you want and why you want it. Be specific, detailed, write it down, visualize it, and feel it as if you already have it. Talk about it and don't let anything drain you of that enthusiasm!

Finally, to transform, decide that you really want to change and commit to changes that will allow a transfiguration. You will need to undertake actions toward it, experience situations, adjust, and change to make sure you are headed in the right direction. Make sure your actions are aligned with your values and life purpose. Be committed, engaged, excited and grateful.

During a transformation, you will undergo rocky moments; there will be times where you may question yourself. Don't give up, be perseverant, believe it is possible, believe you can achieve it, and celebrate each step of the way.

Be flexible, work with what you have, and look for signs. Be ready to suffer — there is always pain involved when we are trying to achieve our goals. If you want to achieve your dreams, consider to be flexible and open to adapt to different environments. You will need to explore and live in uncomfortable situations. The only limits on your life will be the ones that you set yourself. Get out of your comfort zone and explore the new and unknown to liberate your true potential. For that, you should do the things you fear.

- Start by writing down the changes you want in your life from personal, relationship and environmental points of view. List the changes you desire to make and the goals you want to achieve in these three areas.
- The more goals you set, the more you will create the right vibration for your dreams to come true.
- Be precise, positive, present and passionate about it.
- From the personal angle, choose actions to change from physical, emotional, spiritual and intellectual perspectives.
- From the relationship angle, choose actions to change from your personal, romantic, social and professional perspectives.
- From the environmental angle, choose actions to change your environment from personal, shared, social and workspace areas.
- Once you have a detailed list of actions, narrow the list down by crossing out those that don't align with your values and life purpose, and keeping the ones that do.

Once that is done, believe you can achieve what you want. Believe it is possible. Believe you are worth getting what you want. Believe you deserve to get what you want and take action toward all of these goals.

**FREE BONUS VIDEO:**
**"HOW TO CREATE LONG-LASTING CHANGES"**

Discover the keys to making lasting changes and transform your life. In this video you will:
- Learn how to replace limiting beliefs with empowering ones
- Create new habits
- Change your inner world
- Transform your outer reality

Go to www.nathalievirem.com/blog
Life Booster #10: HOW TO CREATE LONG-LASTING CHANGES

## CHAPTER 7 — MASTER YOUR MIND

### I. Self-Esteem

We now have a clear and detailed action plan for you to live with purpose, accomplish your deepest wishes and become the person you want to become. The next step is to build your spirit and faith.

Psychologists have studied self-esteem and its correlation to different parameters. Their findings show that self-esteem has a strong relationship to happiness. As a leader, it will be important that you develop your self-esteem.

Self-esteem is the value you give yourself. It is our own perception. It is how we rate ourselves. It's self-worth, because it is a reflection of how you see yourself.

One's level of self-esteem is a result of how our social context influences what we believe ourselves to be. Therefore, try to be comfortable in your own skin and happy with what you see in the mirror:

- Love and accept yourself.
- Identify your strengths. See the positive in areas you are not so strong in. Transform your weaknesses into strengths and your difficulties into advantages.
- Look at what makes you unique, exceptional, different and irresistible.
- Embrace who you are fully, be yourself, be real, and be authentic to you and others. Don't try to please everybody; you will lose your soul, and nobody will like you. Learn how to say no.
- Be vulnerable: Allow yourself to be the way you are and not the way you want to be. Love yourself for who you are, and don't be afraid to be rejected.

Be a little selfish and think about yourself first by taking care of you, your body and your intellect. Invest in yourself to help form who you are.

Don't spend time comparing yourself to others. Rather, spend time finding yourself and creating who you are.

Don't criticize others or yourself. Be patient, flexible and compassionate; and empathize with others and yourself.

Allow yourself to have low self-esteem at times. Accept that it will happen. After all, it's natural.

You can elevate your self-esteem by:

- Focusing on your values and dreams. Nourish your top values by engaging in your dreams, taking action and risks to reach your goals.
- Taking care of, investing in, and forming yourself.
- Creating your own happiness and being connected to joy.

The exercises listed below will help you build self-esteem:

1. Every morning, look in the mirror and tell yourself that you have value; you are creative, resourceful, whole, magnificent and intelligent. Love yourself and tell yourself how proud you are of who you've become. Love your life, love your trips and love your hobbies.
2. Tell yourself you are worth the time, effort and investment to get what you want.
3. Feel you deserve the reward and recognition that comes with working hard for what you want.
4. Tell yourself: I can do it, I will succeed, I believe in you, I love you and thank you.
5. Use the present tense when performing this exercise.
6. See the universe as a friendly place because you are worth being here.
7. And try not to criticize yourself or others for a week!

**FREE BONUS VIDEO:**
**"HOW TO ELEVATE YOUR SELF-ESTEEM"**

In this video you will learn the secrets to building your self-esteem by uncovering ways to:
- Love and value yourself
- Build spiritual strength
- Develop deep inner faith
- Attain and surpass your goals and dreams

Go to www.nathalievirem.com/blog
Life Booster #11: HOW TO ELEVATE YOUR SELF-ESTEEM

## II. Self-Confidence

Self-confidence is your belief that you can succeed. It is how capable you think you are to accomplish what you want. Self-confidence influences how you take action to obtain what is important for you. It represents trust and faith in oneself. It's your capacity to look at your potential, use it and transform your life. It will allow you to get to a new dimension, to open the doors to a new potential.

One's level of self-confidence is usually a result of overcoming challenges successfully. Several studies conducted since the 1970s have shown that self-confidence is tightly related to an individual's achievements and is a key to success.

Do what you can to reduce the gap between your potential and your results by investing in your personal development with books, audios, videos, training, seminars and courses. Hire a coach; meet people who inspire you, etc. Self-confidence is constructed on solid achievements.

When your why or purpose is very strong, your self-confidence will expand exponentially. You will know exactly what to do. Talk about your dreams; surround yourself with people who have self-confidence and inspire you.

Change your posture: the way you walk, sit, talk and listen. Stand straight, with an open heart and chest. Put your shoulders back, relax the stomach, smile, breathe all the way into your tummy, and close your eyes. And don't forget to laugh and have fun.

Watch the video from Gabrielle Bernstein about "The Power of Your Words." Change your language, and then change the frequency of your stories to those that are more elevated and energizing. Own what you are saying.

Accept the fact that you may never be perfect, but that's not the point. Confidence is about facing obstacles and realizing you're still alive, even when you fail. Be persistent; learn to start better next time.

To be self-confident, practice and get used to do things you are unfamiliar with or scared of, that you find hard, or that give you a certain pain. Take action and go outside your comfort zone. Look at every moment as an opportunity to grow.

Learn to associate the pain, fear and discomfort with pleasure. Self-confidence is a muscle that needs to be used over and over. It grows and evolves as you go. So, try new things; explore and do things that take you out of your comfort zone. Don't fear failure. By failing and getting back onto your feet, you will also expand your self-confidence. Because everything that generates pain and discomfort provides an opportunity in the long run. It is a lesson learned. Remember that everything happens for a reason and that everything is in divine order. Have no regrets — every experience in your life was a learning experience. If you are scared of something you have at heart, do it!

Work with what you have, what you've learned from our previous videos, what you want, why you want it, and what's more important to you now: family, friends, traveling, love, faith...

Define a small action for today, in tune with your vision, why or purpose. Do it even if it's uncomfortable.

Every success needs to be celebrated. Self-confidence is one of the most important muscles for success. Celebrate every victory, every small step.

To build self-confidence:

1. Talk up to yourself out loud; tell yourself and believe you can achieve what you want.
2. Talk about your dreams, and don't let anything drain you of that enthusiasm!

3. Learn to take pleasure in asking for more and learn to say no. Ask for a raise, for a discount, etc. Say no to what no longer feeds your spirit.

4. See what it would be like to not complain for a week and TAKE ACTION. Take the first step. Take a small action, fail, learn, retake another small action and when you succeed, celebrate. Try new things over and over. Take risks. Do something new this week, go to an event or place you haven't been to before, meet new people, or talk to someone you don't usually talk to. Do things that are unknown to you. Commit to eating healthier or exercising more. Take a risk and be uncomfortable.

**FREE BONUS VIDEO:**
**"HOW TO IMPROVE YOUR SELF-CONFIDENCE"**

Learn special techniques to help you:

- Boost your self-confidence
- Believe you can succeed
- Accomplish the goals you set for yourself
- Maximize your potential
- Transform your life

Go to www.nathalievirem.com/blog
Life Booster #12: HOW TO IMPROVE YOUR SELF-CONFIDENCE

### III. Fear of Failure & Stress

Failure is key for entrepreneurship. As an entrepreneur, learn to manage both the fear of failure and stress in order to succeed, as both will be part of your path to success.

If you do nothing, you already have failure.

The fear of failure is strongly related to the volume of failures and the frequency you fail. It's mathematical.

Shift your perception to see failure as a good thing. To develop your capacity to fail (and then succeed), challenge yourself to become the person who is capable of asking anything and all. For example: Ask for that raise you've been waiting for.

Change your language: Be positive, and try not to judge, criticize and devalue yourself and others.

Look for the why: why you want to do it, or why it is important for you, your community or the world. Ask yourself if it is better to not do it and regret it or to do it and maybe fail at it. Remember that the only way to fail is if you never try or if you give up before you succeed!

Remember, it is impossible not to feel fear — we all do. It's one of the ingredients of success. It's part of your life. Fear is needed so that we can protect ourselves. Allow yourself to be scared.
Love fear. Embrace fear and discomfort. If you are afraid of something, do it! Change your perception of fear; look at it from a different angle, from different glasses.

Learn to be conscious when you are afraid. Learn to identify your level of fear (throat, stomach, etc.). Try to control the small signals of fear before the stronger symptoms come (adrenaline, rapid heartbeat, sweaty hands, negative thoughts...).

Visualize yourself being confident with your fear.

Surround yourself with people who like fear. People who are cool with it and get pleasure from it.

Fear is your path to success. Learn to transform fear with power. Fear guides you. If you don't feel ready, it is best to take a small step. Visualize yourself taking that small step. Visualize yourself succeeding when taking that small step. Visualize yourself celebrating that victory.

The same goes with stress. Learn to see stress as an opportunity. Changing the perspective will help you remove negative feelings and consequently will change your outer reality

To handle stress, learn how to breathe: Start by focusing on the stomach, then breathe in deeply and fill in your stomach completely, like a balloon. Learn to observe the physical symptoms of stress. Detach yourself from the emotions, try not to judge and just observe.

Here are some techniques to better manage fear and stress:

1. Extract the stress or fear to outside of your body.
2. Hold that fear or stress in your hands, and then look at it from afar.
3. Breathe softly and deeply from your stomach.
4. Stand straight, with your heart open and your shoulders back, and smile.

Watch Marie Forleo's video, "Fear vs. Intuition: How To Tell The Difference." Afterwards, ask your natural knowing, "Do you feel expansive or contracted?" If you answer expansive, in forward motion, then yes, go for it! If you feel contracted or pooled in, then no, don't do it.

**FREE BONUS VIDEO:
"HOW TO MANAGE FEAR OF FAILURE & STRESS"**

Learn how to shift your experience so you can:
- Embrace failure, allowing you to progress faster
- Learn to manage stress
- Feel fear without being disabled by it, and empower yourself to move forward
- Ask for what you want and get it

You will discover techniques designed to help you better manage your fear of failure and stress.

Go to www.nathalievirem.com/blog
Life Booster #13: HOW TO MANAGE FEAR OF FAILURE & STRESS

### IV. Courage & Vulnerability

To better face your fear of failure, embrace vulnerability. If you dare to help make the world a better place, courage will be instrumental. Be courageous to be who you are, to accomplish your mission in this world, to show your feelings, and to talk about your deepest desires. Give yourself permission to be who you are, to be loved for who you really are, for your uniqueness. Give yourself permission to dream big, beyond what you think you could ever achieve or become. See the possible where others see the impossible. What if it were possible? Why is it important to you? Does it resonate with you?

Expect to be rejected for who you are and what you believe in. Chances are you will sense a pushback from your loved ones and friends. This happens because your loved ones and friends are scared of the challenges you have set for yourself, and they don't have the courage to take on those challenges themselves. It's natural; they will tell you that it's unrealistic, yet they will observe you from afar. You will sense a lack of cheering and support. The more you sense people are cynical about what you are trying to achieve, the more you should trust that you are headed in the right direction. You know you are not here to survive, you are here to thrive, and to thrive you should take risks and action.

Once you are clear on the inside, everything is possible outside; it will be easier to be courageous and open to vulnerability. Know what you want and why you want it first. The how is unknown, what matters is the why. The why will create a vibration that will trigger your nervous system.

Your nervous system will then select the information around you, the behaviors to develop, and the lessons to learn in order to heal and better yourself as a human being. Once these elements combine and fall into place, you'll be ready to undertake your mission and approach the circles you need to interact with in order to become the person you want to become and achieve the results you want to achieve.

Be ready to suffer and encounter pain on the path to fulfillment. Look carefully at the price you may have to pay for your dreams to come true. There is always a price to pay. Most people want success, fame and power, and when they have it they are not willing to give up their personal life publicly, nor do they want to give up time with their loved ones. For that, ensure that why you want something is in perfect alignment with your values, purpose and heart.

Have the courage to take action. Do things that you don't know how to do and be strong.

Be vulnerable: Admit when you are scared, mad or have doubts, and talk about your areas of improvement, your struggles and obstacles.

Engage yourself one hundred percent in what you believe in and who you are. Decide to take action and don't worry about others. Do everything you can to make it happen. The world is in your hands, so decide what is important to you. Take charge of your life. TAKE ACTION. Nothing will happen if you don't take action. Take small steps to start and validate that they are working. After that, take radical actions to make long-lasting changes that will help you realize your dreams.

It is impossible to expect a different result if we do the same thing over and over again. Therefore, you need to change the formula, do new things, go to new places, and speak to people you are not used to talking to.

Watch the TEDx Talk video "The Power of Vulnerability" from Dr. Brené Brown, who has spent over a decade studying vulnerability and courage. In this video, she explains how vulnerability is the birthplace of Innovation, Creativity and Change. To watch the video, go to www.ted.com/talks/brene_brown_on_vulnerability.

**FREE BONUS VIDEO:**
**"HOW TO EMBRACE COURAGE & VULNERABILITY"**

Learn how to achieve your purpose and goals by:
- Discovering how to be vulnerable in a way that helps you grow
- Uncovering the courage to be who you are and take action
- Been able to feel vulnerable to unleash the power of creativity
- Living authentically from your true purpose

You'll get some quick tips to help you embrace courage and vulnerability

Go to www.nathalievirem.com/blog
Life Booster #14: HOW TO EMBRACE COURAGE & VULNERABILITY

### V. Mind Mastering

We become what we think about and we attract what we think about. Read the book *The Strangest Secret* by Earl Nightingale. You are today the result of what you thought of and the actions you took in the past.

Focus on what you want, not what you don't. Give your undivided attention to the things that you want. Think about your goals and desires every morning. Don't put any attention or energy into the things you don't want in your life. Be pro-something. When you see things that you don't want in your life, don't talk or write about them, but don't push against them either. Instead, let them be, let emotions flow and give attention to the things that you want instead.

It is proven that a new attitude, positive or negative, sends new messages to the cells and reprograms our cellular structure's health and behavior. When we think positively, we can turn diseased cells into healthy cells.

The medical field calls it the "placebo effect," where people have been known to heal themselves based purely on their thoughts. Patients are led to believe the medication they're taking will cure their ailments, but unbeknownst to them, the "medication" is fake. Rather than the medicine curing the patient, it is their belief that the placebo is working that provides a cure. It is not the "medicine," but the power of their minds that actually heal them. The key is in your thoughts. The human mind is the biggest factor in the healing process, sometimes more than the drugs provided. Today, there are several studies that prove this placebo effect (or the power of consciousness).

Visualize constantly what you want as if you already have it. Visualize, visualize, visualize. It will not work if you only do it once. Believe that it is possible to create the world you want while allowing the world that others choose to be in to also exist. When you dream big, you change the way you think, you change your nervous system, and you create pleasure and find solutions naturally. The key resides in your thoughts. If you can control your thoughts by focusing them on what you want and dream of, it will be possible and become a reality. Your thoughts are vital. Feel the emotions you will feel when you have what you want as if you already have it.

Change negative thoughts into positive ones. When you have a negative thought, try flipping it into a positive thought. When the negative thought is about something, rather than someone, it is usually easier to change that thought into a positive one. It gets harder when the negative thoughts come from someone you dislike or are arguing with. Here is a tip to help you do your best to change that negative thought: Make a list of the positive things about people you may not be on positive terms with. Try to see the good in them, the positive in them, so that if you ever see each other again and they are in a mood or have an attitude that doesn't match yours, your frequencies will be unaligned, and conflict won't exist.

Learn to be in the present moment, in the now. As Eckhart Tolle says, "Realize deeply that the present moment is all you have. Make the NOW the primary focus of your life."

Mr. Tolle goes further by saying, "As soon as you honor the present moment, all unhappiness and struggle dissolve, and life begins to flow with joy and ease. When you act out the present-moment awareness, whatever you do becomes imbued with a sense of quality, care, and love — even the simplest action."

Another tip Eckhart Tolle offers is to "Watch any plant or animal and let it teach you acceptance of what is, surrender to the Now."

To positively change the world, push yourself to go beyond. Challenge yourself to literally move to a different dimension. Have the mind, the energy, the perspective and the spirit of an Olympic champion.

Go for the extra push and give the extra effort. Be persistent, recurrent and regular. Improve, adjust and practice, practice, practice. Magic will come when you surpass yourself.

Make meditation part of your life. Meditation has been proven to not only offer health benefits, but to also help people change their brain structure by creating new neural pathways.

Purchase and complete Deepak Chopra's 21-Day Meditation Experience™ by going to www.chopracentermeditation.com. Remember that miracles don't exist. You manifest everything that happens in your life. Your dreams come true because you created the energy for them to exist.

You are the only one who can think for yourself.

> "All that we are is the result of what we have thought."
>
> —Buddha

If you need support on helping you move forward, visit www.nathalievirem.com/contact to schedule a 'mind mastery' free session where we would work together to uncover what is blocking you from moving forward.

**FREE BONUS VIDEO: "HOW TO MASTER YOUR MIND"**

Mind mastery is instrumental for success and sustainability. In this video, you will learn to:
- Become aware of your beliefs, thoughts and words
- Change beliefs that don't serve you
- Attract and manifest what you desire

Go to www.nathalievirem.com/blog
Life Booster #16: HOW TO MASTER YOUR MIND

# CHAPTER 8 — POSITIVE, LASTING CHANGE

## I. Success

Success is personal. To take that first step toward success, identify what success means to you personally. It is different for everybody. Not everyone wants the same things.

Success comes from within; it is the result of your authentic voice. A voice aligned with your values and purpose. When you express yourself from your true inner voice, you can't help but to succeed. Once your inner voice and purpose are clear, you have mastered your life.

We exist to create the world that we choose and also to allow others to create the world that they choose to exist. Because life is limitless and abundant, and there are limitless resources for all of us to succeed.

As we learned earlier in this book, the first step to success is exploration. That is, to be clear and specific on what you want and why you want it. Self-exploration takes into consideration your values, environment, life purpose, business purpose and how they all link together.

To make your purpose a reality, try to visualize. Visualize it as if you already have what you wanted and observe how you feel when visualizing having what you want. Make the desire a burning desire so that you can take action with discipline and enthusiasm.

Once you are clear on why you are here — your life purpose, and why your business exists — it's time to take action with short- and long-term goals toward the realization of what you want. To be successful, learn how to make decisions. To succeed, consider being fully engaged in what you want to succeed in. So, get involved!

Take risks, experience new things. Pick experiences that will bring quality to your success, and trigger these experiences often. The more you experience, the more you will develop and progress. Then learn from every experience. What did I learn? What would I do differently next time? Spend some time appraising your progress. At the end of the day, think of what you accomplished and what you would do differently tomorrow. Be self-aware of your missteps and make immediate improvements based on what your learned from them.

Success usually takes several steps. First you may have to fail, and then learn from the experience, and then be able to change the equation until you ultimately succeed. Failure is temporary; when purpose comes to you and you are passionate about what you do, you will ultimately succeed. Obstacles that present themselves during the journey will give you valuable lessons to prepare for success. Learn to change the questions you usually ask yourself and others.

Surround yourself with people who inspire you and have the ability to succeed the way you want to succeed yourself. Model yourself after them by liberating what you already have in yourself. Read their biographies to better understand what makes them a success.

Trust others. Give them value. Give them the opportunity to change and succeed the way you want to succeed.

Finally, talk about what you want over and over and over again. Learn to talk about what you value, what matters to you.

People who know what they want and why they want it, who have goals set toward accomplishing what they want, and who are capable of talking about what they want are those who succeed the fastest.

Get clear on why you want what you want, take action toward it, fail, change and don't give up until you succeed.

This is what I challenge you to do this week:

#1. Clarify why it is important for you to take certain actions.

#2. Take an action toward what you want to accomplish.

#3. Look back at the action you took and let me know what you've learned from it, and what you would do differently next time. Read the books *The Success Principles* by Jack Canfield and *The Seven Spiritual Laws of Success* by Deepak Chopra.

Send this to: contact@nathalievirem.com. I will invite you to a complimentary discovery free session to define your plan for success.

**FREE BONUS VIDEO: "HOW TO SUCCEED"**

Decision making is essential for success. Learn to make powerful decisions by turning on your ability to:
- Be fully engaged
- Be deeply involved
- Be ready to take action
- Understand why failure leads to success
- Stick it out until you hit your target

In this video, you will also learn several techniques to enhance your likelihood of success.

Go to www.nathalievirem.com/blog
Life Booster #15: HOW TO SUCCEED

### II. Quantum Leaps

Quantum leaps will help you accelerate success.

In quantum physics, a particular state shifts to a different state instantaneously, radically. After a quantum leap, you will perceive opportunities that you were unable to perceive before. You are accessing a new dimension. You are now seeing things from a different mindset, and the opportunities become clearer and multiply themselves.

Here are some ways to trigger a quantum leap:

1. First, when you experience new things. If you do the same things over and over, you will experience a linear growth, but not a quantum leap. Therefore, think about doing things that scare you, that seem too big, too challenging. The higher you get, the closer you will get to a new dimension. To trigger a quantum leap, be opened to continuously transform new challenges into opportunities. A consciousness grows. As you accomplish this, you will see how what you thought was difficult, now that you are able to accomplish it, becomes less challenging. You no longer see things the same way or in the same frequency; you become a new person. And your next challenge will be bigger than the one you just accomplished, which now feels small.

2. Your mind shapes the dimension you live in. Today you are the thoughts, feelings and behaviors of your past. Your past behaviors determine your current success. Consider shifting the thoughts and feelings you have about certain experiences if you want to change the chemistry of your body and create new behaviors — and ultimately a new destiny.

3. Your limbic system travels through time. Visualize the life you want and feel it. Your nervous system will then create some neurological connections to change the chemistry of your body. Think about your dreams and feel them as if you already achieved them. The more you feel them, the more you will become the person you want to become. With that chemistry, think about the behaviors, thoughts and beliefs a person needs to have if they want to achieve those dreams.

### III. Giving Back

To receive, give.

To make money, invest.

To be loved, love.

To be trusted, trust.

To inspire, feel inspired.

That is the Law of Cause and Effect: Whatever you give, you will receive. It's a give-and-take equation. You can't take without giving.

Therefore, when you succeed, you will need to give back in return to sustain that success. You were granted success for a reason. It is your responsibility to give back in return what was given to you.

Once you succeed, become the lighthouse for others to also succeed. First you will have to get there. And once you get there, then you should be able to send light back to help others get there.

The Law of Cause and Effect is not a new concept. Read the book *The Game of Life and How to Play It* by Florence Scovel Shinn. First published in 1925, this book explains the key to life, which we now refer to as the Law of Cause and Effect, Karma, or giving and receiving. The author states that life is a game about giving and receiving. Today, it's more than a game — it's the key to success. It is important to understand that what we put out in the world, whether it is a thought or action, will be returned to us and will affect the quality of our lives.

**CONCLUSION — LIVE WITH PURPOSE**

Live with purpose. As Abraham Maslow said, "Musicians must make music, artists must paint, poets must write if they are to be ultimately at peace with themselves. What human beings can be, they must be. They must be true to their own nature. This need we may call self-actualization... It refers to man's desire for self-fulfillment, namely to the tendency for him to become actually what he is potentially: to become everything one is capable of becoming."

Become everything you are capable of becoming and you will find eternal joy. And trust that when purpose comes to you, the world will eventually change.

That is what I hope you do. I hope you realize your purpose so that you can assist others in achieving their purpose in return. If you read this book, you were called to serve others with purpose.

As I mentioned at the beginning of this book, every path to achieving a purpose-driven life is unique, and some have harder or longer journeys than others. Now that you have read the book, take a daily approach to the strategies I have shared with you to guarantee success in creating positive, lasting change in the world.

With these final words, I surrender. My book is my gift to you, visionary. It's now time for me to let go and trust that everything will happen for you, as it should.

## ACKNOWLEDGEMENTS

To those who live with purpose.

The dreamers. The alchemists. The nonconformists.

You believe in the impossible.

You have no patience for "No."

And you have no tolerance for limiting beliefs.

You may be respected, argued against, admired or defamed.

But you won't disappear.

Because you are made of infinite power, love and energy.

You are the inventors and creators of everything.

And while others perceive you as the foolish ones,
I see magicians.

Because those who live with purpose, are the ones who
redefine the human kind.

Live with purpose.

Nathalie Virem
***Live With Purpose***
www.nathalievirem.com

www.ingramcontent.com/pod-product-compliance
Lightning Source LLC
Chambersburg PA
CBHW070516090426
42735CB00012B/2808